HORSING AROUND

Show Jumping

Robin Johnson

Crabtree Publishing Company

www.crabtreebooks.com

Crabtree Publishing Company

www.crabtreebooks.com

Author: Robin Johnson
Editor: Lynn Peppas
Proofreader: Crystal Sikkens
Editorial director: Kathy Middleton
Production coordinator: Katherine Berti
Prepress technician: Katherine Berti
Coordinating editor: Chester Fisher
Series editor: Sue Labella
Project manager: Kumar Kunal (Q2AMEDIA)
Art direction: Dibakar Acharjee (Q2AMEDIA)
Cover design: Shruti Aggarwal (Q2AMEDIA)
Design: Shruti Aggarwal (Q2AMEDIA)
Photo research: Ekta Sharma (Q2AMEDIA)
Reading consultant: Cecilia Minden, Ph.D.

Cover: A horse and rider clear a fence
at a show-jumping competition.

Title page: A horse and rider make their
way through a show-jumping course.

Illustrations:
Q2AMedia Art Bank : P22

Photographs:
Cover: Daniele La Monaca/Photolibrary (main image),
Emberiza/Shutterstock, Tischenko Irina/Shutterstock,
P1: Kondrashov Mikhail Evgenevich/Shutterstock,
P4: Mikhail Kondrashov/ Istockphoto, P5: Jean-Yves
Ruszniewski/ TempSport/Corbis, P6: Bettmann/
Corbis P7: Library of Congress, P8: Hedda Gjerpen/
Istockphoto, P9: Hedda Gjerpen/Istockphoto, P10:
Margo Harrison/Shutterstock, P11: Kit Houghton/
Corbis, P12: Daniele La Monaca/Photolibrary, P13:
Desmond Boylan/Reuters, P14: Ahmed Jadallah/
Reuters, P15: Hedda Gjerpen/Istockphoto, P16:
Robert Zolles/Reuters, P17: Bobby Yip/Reuters,
P18: Abramova Kseniya/ Shutterstock, P19: Jeff R.
Clow/Shutterstock, P20: Kondrashov MIkhail
Evgenevich/Shutterstock, P21: Dreamstime, P23:
Hedda Gjerpen/Istockphoto, P24: Bob Langrish/
Getty Images, P25: Christof Koepsel/Bongarts/
Getty Images, P26: Gary Hershorn/Corbis, P27:
George Silk/Time & Life Pictures/Getty Images,
P28: Thomas Kienzle/Associated Press, P29: Tish
Quirk, P30: Interfoto/Alamy, P31: Susan Walsh/
Associated Press, Folio Image: Wendy Kaveney
Photography/Shutterstock

Library and Archives Canada Cataloguing in Publication

Johnson, Robin (Robin R.)
    Show jumping / Robin Johnson.

(Horsing around)
Includes index.
ISBN 978-0-7787-4979-0 (bound).--ISBN 978-0-7787-4995-0 (pbk.)

    1. Show jumping--Juvenile literature. I. Title. II. Series: Horsing around
(St. Catharines, Ont.)

SF295.525.J64 2009   j798.2'5079   C2009-903881-1

Library of Congress Cataloging-in-Publication Data

Johnson, Robin (Robin R.)
    Show jumping / Robin R. Johnson.
      p. cm. -- (Horsing around)
    Includes index.
    ISBN 978-0-7787-4995-0 (pbk. : alk. paper) -- ISBN 978-0-7787-4979-0
(reinforced library binding : alk. paper)
    1. Show jumping--Juvenile literature. 2. Show horses--Training--Juvenile
literature. 3. Show jumpers (Persons)--Juvenile literature. I. Title. II. Series.

SF295.525.J65 2009
798.2'5079--dc22

                                                          2009024755

Crabtree Publishing Company

www.crabtreebooks.com   1-800-387-7650

Published in Canada
Crabtree Publishing
616 Welland Ave.
St. Catharines, ON
L2M 5V6

Published in the United States
Crabtree Publishing
PMB16A
350 Fifth Ave., Suite 3308
New York, NY 10118

Published in the United Kingdom
Crabtree Publishing
Maritime House
Basin Road North, Hove
BN41 1WR

Published in Australia
Crabtree Publishing
386 Mt. Alexander Rd.
Ascot Vale (Melbourne)
VIC 3032

Contents

Chapter	Title	Page
1	Show Jumping 101	4
2	Show Jumping History	6
3	Courses for Horses	8
4	The Jumps	10
5	What's the Score?	12
6	The Competitions	14
7	Grand Prix Events	16
8	The Best Breeds	18
9	Jumping for Joy	20
10	The Equipment	22
11	Dressed for Success	24
12	Show Jumping Horses	26
13	Show Jumping Riders	28
	Facts and Figures	30
	Glossary and Index	32

Show Jumping 101

Show jumping is an **equestrian** sport. In show-jumping events, horses and riders try to jump a number of obstacles. They move together through difficult courses. They work to be fast and exact.

Horses and riders around the world compete on show-jumping courses. The courses are made up of many obstacles. These include fences, gates, walls, and water jumps. Show jumping is also called stadium jumping or jumpers.

Show-jumping riders can take part in events as individuals or as teams. In individual events, a rider and horse move quickly through a series of difficult jumps and turns.

Show jumpers must have speed, control, and a lot of horse power.

This rider is hoping to win a bright ribbon at a colorful show-jumping event.

They try to make as few mistakes as possible. In team events, the scores of a team of riders are added together. The team with the best score wins.

Show jumping can be compared to dressage. In dressage, horses learn to perform specific moves. The horses get little direction from their riders. In show jumping, horses must be able to make quick, sharp turns and change their leading legs. They must angle their bodies through jumps, and perform other dressage skills.

FACT BOX

Show-jumping events are exciting, colorful shows. They have brightly painted obstacles on fancy courses. Riders often wear red jackets at top events. They compete for bright ribbons. The best jumpers usually receive blue or red ribbons.

5

Show Jumping History

People have jumped horses over fences and other obstacles for years. Competitive show jumping grew from the sport of fox hunting in England and France. Over time, it became a sport that fans enjoyed. They watched skilled athletes complete difficult courses in arenas.

In England, in the 1700s and 1800s, people built fences to protect their property. Fox hunters on horseback once rode freely through the fields. When the fences appeared, riders began jumping them. Soon, the hunters were competing with one another as they jumped fences across the fields. In 1866, the first show-jumping contest was held in Paris, France. Riders and horses walked in a parade in front of fans. Then they left to jump over fences in the countryside. The fans were not able to watch the contests in the open fields.

Early riders used horses to jump fences and chase foxes in fields. Today, riders chase prizes in show-jumping events.

Soon, jumping events with obstacles began to take place in enclosed arenas. This way, spectators could enjoy the shows.

The first international show-jumping contest was held in 1902. The sport was called leaping. It was dominated for many years by military officers. The officers were well trained to use horses in battle.

This military officer and his horse are taking on an early show-jumping course.

Once tanks and trucks began to be used in battle, fewer officers were trained to jump horses. Other jumpers then began to compete as well.

FACT BOX

Early show-jumping courses were very different from courses today. The sport began with a few simple jumps. Fences were often single rails. Horses would often duck under the fences instead of jumping over them!

Courses for Horses

Show-jumping events today take place on difficult courses built in arenas. The look and position of the obstacles are important. These can affect how a horse and rider perform. While all courses must follow certain rules, each course is different.

There are 10 to 13 jumps in high-level show-jumping courses. Each jump is numbered. Jumps must be completed in the correct order. A course's starting line is marked with the letter S.

The finish line is marked with the letter F. The starting line, finish line, and jumps on a course are marked with flags. Red flags are set on the right and white flags on the

This horse and rider are headed up and over!

left. Riders must pass between the flags at each stage of the course. Riders who miss the flags or go through in the wrong direction are disqualified from the event.

Riders walk through the courses before a show-jumping event. They plan how many **strides** their horses should take between jumps. They look for any possible problems or dangers.

Riders also plan the best takeoff points for jumps. A horse that is too far from an obstacle at takeoff could land near the obstacle. That might cause the horse to knock down a rail with its back legs. If a horse is too close to an obstacle at takeoff, it might hit a rail with its front legs.

FACT BOX

Show-jumping courses can sometimes be a little too tricky! The course at the 1932 Olympics was so difficult that no team completed it. No medals were given in the team show-jumping event that year.

This rider prepares for competition by walking through a difficult show-jumping course.

The Jumps

There are five main types of obstacles in show-jumping events: verticals, spreads, combinations, walls, and water jumps. All obstacles have parts that may be knocked down by horses. Each obstacle is designed to test horses and riders in different ways.

Verticals are jumps that have several poles or planks lined up one above the other. They are the most difficult jumps. Fences and gates are vertical jumps. Spreads are wide obstacles. They are made up of two or more low verticals placed close together.

Combinations are made up of two or three obstacles in a row. These are placed one or two steps apart. Jumps with two obstacles are called double combinations.

Rails rest in shallow cups. They are designed to fall easily without harming horses or riders.

This young rider is using ground poles to learn how to jump.

Jumps with three obstacles are triple combinations. A horse and rider may miss an obstacle when jumping a combination. Then they must complete the entire jump again.

Walls are obstacles that look like solid brick or stone walls. They are not solid. They are made of light materials and can easily be broken. Water jumps have low areas of water. They may have low fences or hedges in front of them. Their landing sides are shown with white strips called laths. Horses must get past the laths to complete the jump.

5 What's the Score?

Riders aim for fast and perfect jumps. Winners may be the jumpers with the fewest mistakes. They could also have the fastest time, or the most points.

Show jumpers win competitions by completing clear rounds. A clear round is a perfect ride in which no rails are knocked down. Style doesn't matter in show-jumping events. All that matters is completing the courses cleanly and quickly.

All obstacles on a course must be jumped in a set amount of time. Time limits are set according to the size of the courses. Pairs who exceed the time limit receive penalty points. They may also have time added to their scores.

Even the world's best riders sometimes fall during a competition.

Show jumpers receive faults if they make mistakes during competitions. Faults are scoring penalties. Show jumpers are given faults for knocking down any parts of obstacles that affect height. For example, jumpers receive faults for knocking down the top rails of vertical jumps. They do not get faults for knocking down bottom or middle rails. No faults are given for touching an obstacle that does not fall.

Riders also receive faults if their horses balk, or refuse to jump. Balking is when a horse stops in front of an obstacle or goes around it. If a horse balks twice, the pair is removed from the event. Pairs are also disqualified if the rider, horse, or both fall during a show-jumping event.

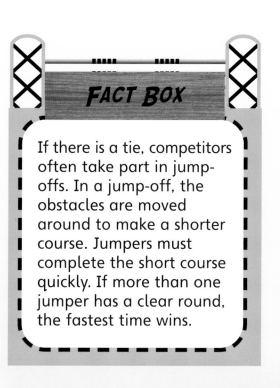

FACT BOX

If there is a tie, competitors often take part in jump-offs. In a jump-off, the obstacles are moved around to make a shorter course. Jumpers must complete the short course quickly. If more than one jumper has a clear round, the fastest time wins.

This pair has knocked down rails in a show-jumping event. They will receive a costly fault for their mistake.

6

The Competitions

Men, women, and children take part in show-jumping competitions around the world. The competitions are different in size, skill level, and events. They are all exciting shows of talent.

Some show-jumping events are small. They are local horse shows for amateur riders. Amateurs are people who play their sport for fun. These show-jumping events are for people of all ages and skill levels. They give riders the opportunity to show their talents and improve their skills. They can meet other show jumpers, and have fun, too!

There are also huge national or international events. These are for professional riders. Professionals are paid to play their sports. Riders compete for cash prizes.

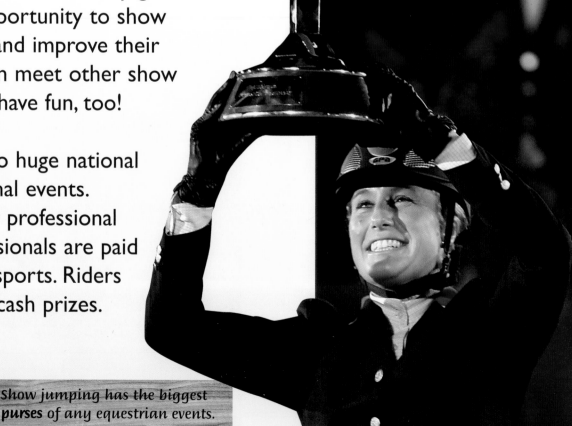

Show jumping has the biggest **purses** of any equestrian events.

Many professional show-jumping events are held each year.

Some show-jumping competitions consist of only individual and team events. Others include several equestrian events. Show jumpers often compete in equestrian competitions called eventing. Eventing is a sport made up of show jumping, dressage, and cross-country. Cross-country is an event with racers who jump. They leap large, natural-looking obstacles such as logs and ditches on open land. Eventing tests the skill and **stamina** of competitors.

Many show jumpers begin training at an early age. It takes years of practice and hard work to master the sport.

FACT BOX

Some horse shows include events such as puissance. Puissance means power. In this event, horses and riders jump high walls. After each round, the walls are made higher. Puissance walls often become more than 7 feet (2.1 m) high!

Grand Prix Events

Grand Prix events are the most difficult and important show-jumping competitions. Few riders can complete these events with clear rounds. Those who can are declared the best show jumpers in the world.

The **FEI** World Equestrian Games is thought by many riders to be the most important event in show jumping. The Games take place every four years between the Summer Olympics.

In 2010, they will take place in Kentucky, U.S.A. Other Grand Prix events include the FEI World Cup and the FEI Nations Cup. The World Cup is a group of indoor competitions that are held every year.

This horse and rider are in grand form at a Grand Prix show-jumping event.

At the 2008 Olympics, Canadian Eric Lamaze and Hickstead won the individual show-jumping competition. It was Canada's first gold medal in the event.

The top jumper is crowned at the World Cup. The Nations Cup is the oldest and most important team jumping competition in the world.

Show jumping is also part of the Olympic Games. It is one of three equestrian events held at the Olympics. The others are dressage and eventing. Show jumping has been on the Olympic program since 1912. Women were not allowed to compete in show jumping until 1956. Today, men and women compete equally in Olympic and other show-jumping events.

FACT BOX

The 1956 Olympics were held in Australia. However, show jumping and other equestrian events took place five months earlier in Sweden! Australia had strict **quarantine** laws at the time. They would not allow horses from other countries into Australia.

The Best Breeds

Horses competing in show-jumping events are strong, fast, and athletic. They have good balance and work well with their riders. They also have the skill and courage to go over large obstacles in a single leap.

Many breeds of horses are successful in show jumping. Most jumpers are tall horses, but not all tall horses are good jumpers. Thoroughbreds are often show-jumping horses. **Warmbloods** are also skilled jumpers. Trakehners (Tra-ka-nur) and Hanoverians (Ha-nuh-vir-ee-un) are warmbloods that are often used in show jumping.

Even horses that are built for jumping must be taught the skills they need. Riders begin training horses by taking them over ground poles. Ground poles help teach horses balance, coordination, and the jumping movements.

mane

withers

tail

hoof

Thoroughbreds are tall, slim, and fast horses.

Trainers often use lunge lines to help teach their horses to jump. Lunge lines are long straps that allow trainers to control their horses from a distance.

Riders then jump the horses over low rails. They increase the size and difficulty of the jumps over time.

Horses are trained slowly to build up their strength and skill. The best jumpers spend more time learning dressage skills than they do jumping, however. Grand Prix riders usually train with other horses and save their best jumpers for competitions. Horses must be well groomed, or cleaned, for show-jumping events. Riders groom their horses by carefully washing and brushing their coats. They braid the manes and tails of

their horses for a neat, clean look. They paint their horses' hoofs with oil to make them shine.

FACT BOX

Horses are measured in hands from their hoofs to their withers. A hand is four inches (10 cm) long. Most show-jumping horses are over 16 hands. Some as small as 14 hands have successfully competed in Grand Prix events. In fact, a **pony** named Stroller that stood just 14.2 hands won the silver medal at the 1968 Olympics!

Jumping for Joy

Riders must communicate with their horses to jump over obstacles successfully. They must maintain good balance and proper positions through the five steps of a jump.

Step 1: The Approach

A rider should approach the center of a jump in a normal riding position. He or she should be sitting up and looking straight ahead. The rider should not be looking at the jump. The rider must feel secure. If the horse senses a rider is not ready to jump, it will stop short in front of the obstacle.

Step 2: The Take-Off

The horse decides when to jump. As it takes off, the rider leans forward with a straight back. The rider raises his or her behind from the saddle. He or she gently squeezes the sides of the horse with his or her knees.

This horse and rider are working together to jump over obstacles in a show-jumping course.

Step 3: The Moment Of Suspension

As the horse is in the air above the obstacle, the rider's arms are stretched forward. This helps balance the rider's body on the horse. The rider's weight is on his or her heels.

Step 4: The Landing

During the landing, the rider looks ahead to the next jump. He or she gently returns to a sitting position in the saddle.

Step 5: The Getaway

After the horse lands, the horse and rider become balanced again. The rider and horse move away from the jump. The rider prepares for the next obstacle in the course.

FACT BOX

Captain Federico Caprilli is considered "the father of modern riding." Caprilli was an Italian equestrian who studied the movements of jumping horses. He developed the forward **seat** that is used today. The forward seat is the riding position explained on these pages. It allows horses to jump obstacles naturally and comfortably.

Beginners should take lessons with trained instructors and experienced horses to learn proper skills before trying to jump.

The Equipment

Show jumping requires special tack, or riding equipment. The tack helps riders to stay on their horses as they move quickly through courses and jump over high obstacles.

Show jumpers use a forward, flat style of English saddle. Jumping saddles are held in place with strong straps called breastplates and girths. Many girths have belly guards to protect the horses from shoe studs when they jump (see box). Saddles rest on thick pads that help keep the saddles clean.

In international show jumping, saddle pads are usually white and square. Riders put their feet in stirrups. These are attached to the saddle. The stirrups in show jumping are shorter than in other equestrian events.

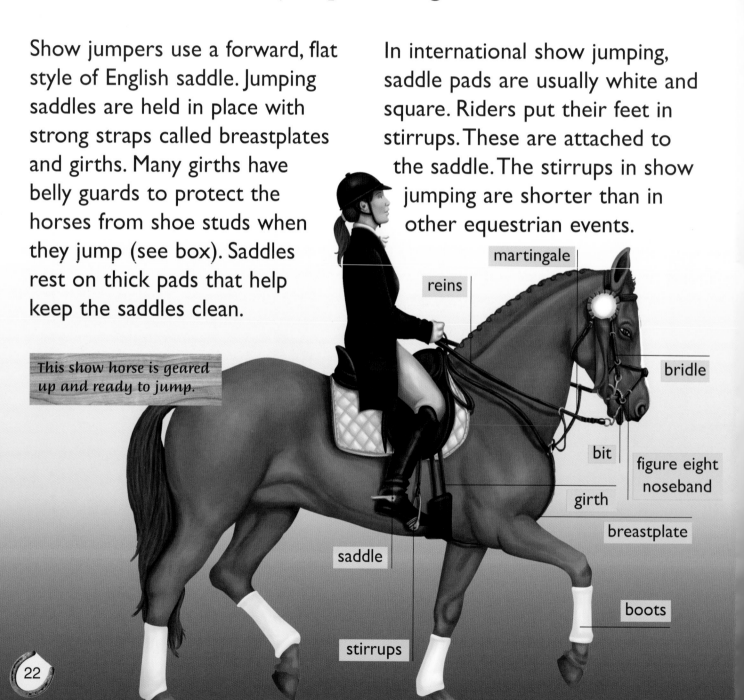

This show horse is geared up and ready to jump.

martingale

reins

bridle

bit

figure eight noseband

girth

breastplate

saddle

boots

stirrups

Jumping saddles allow riders to lean forward, move freely, and use safe jumping positions.

Short stirrups allow riders to lift their behinds off the saddles when they jump. Riders hold onto non-slip reins. Reins allow riders to guide and control their horses. Most show jumpers attach running martingales to the reins. Martingales are straps that keep horses from lifting their heads too high.

A bridle is a series of straps that fit around a horse's head. Bits and nosebands are parts of bridles.

A bit is a piece that fits in the horse's mouth. It is attached to the reins. A noseband is a strap that is around the horse's nose and jaw. Most show jumpers use figure-eight nosebands. These can make it easier for a horse to breathe.

11 Dressed for Success

Riders work hard and train for many years to become skilled show jumpers. Once they learn how to ride and jump, they can begin competing. Just like horses, riders at show-jumping events must be very well groomed.

This rider is dressed to impress and ready for success.

During show-jumping events, riders wear dressy clothing. Both men and women wear white shirts and white ties around their necks. They wear dark-colored jackets that are usually navy blue or black. In Grand Prix events, riders often wear red jackets. Riders wear white or tan breeches. Breeches are tight-fitting pants. Riders who are in the military usually wear their uniforms during competitions. All riders must wear hard hats with chin straps to protect their heads. Some also wear safety vests. Riders wear tall, polished riding boots with low heels. The heels help keep the riders' feet from slipping out of the stirrups. Some riders wear gloves to help them hold the reins.

Riders carry short whips. In show-jumping events, the whips cannot be longer than 30 inches (75 cm). Most show-jumping riders also wear pointed objects called spurs on the heels of their boots. Riders use whips and spurs to encourage their horses to move. If riders use whips and spurs correctly, they do not harm the horses.

FACT BOX

Riders are not judged on their appearance in show-jumping events. However, it is still important for them to look neat and tidy. Riders with long hair should braid their hair or tuck it under their hats. Competitors' clothes should be clean and neat. Riders do not usually wear flashy or colorful clothing.

Spectators are seeing red as this rider competes in a Grand Prix show-jumping event.

Show Jumping Horses

Show jumpers are some of the most talented athletes in the world. Their riders are pretty good, too! These pages show some of the most beloved four-legged competitors in the sport of show jumping.

Touch of Class was a 16-hand **bay** Thoroughbred. She had a short racing career, then became a skilled show jumper. Touch of Class became the first horse ever to complete double clear rounds in Olympic competition. She jumped 90 out of 91 obstacles at the Games. She won gold medals in both the individual and team show-jumping events! Touch of Class was given the Female Equestrian Athlete of the Year Award. It was the first time a horse ever won the prize!

Touch of Class was a first-class show jumper. Here she jumps her way to Olympic victory—and a place in the record books.

Snowman was a popular jumping horse in the 1950s and 1960s. He won numerous awards and show-jumping competitions. Fans loved Snowman for his calm nature and his talent.

He was so gentle, even children could ride him! He was even willing to jump over other horses! In 1992, Snowman was inducted, or admitted as a member, into the Show Jumping Hall of Fame.

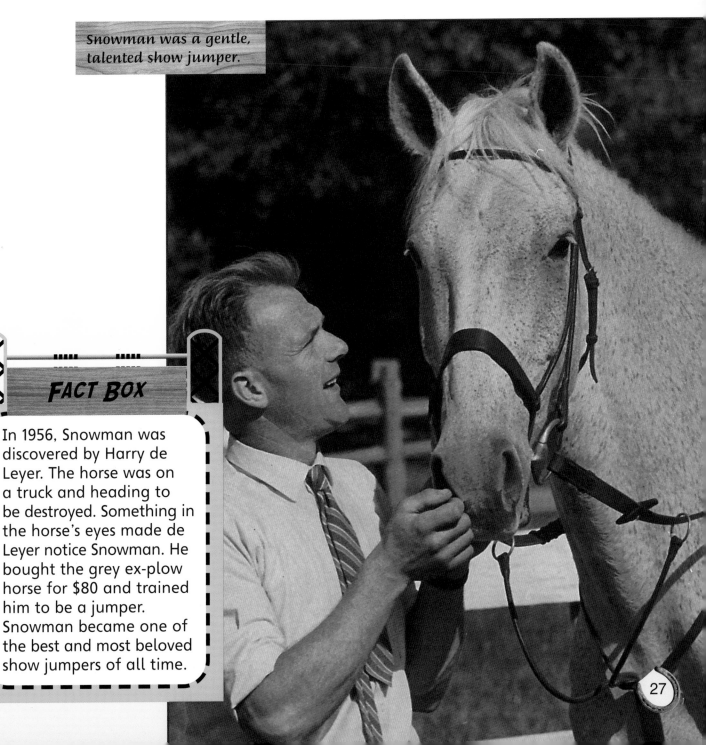

Snowman was a gentle, talented show jumper.

FACT BOX

In 1956, Snowman was discovered by Harry de Leyer. The horse was on a truck and heading to be destroyed. Something in the horse's eyes made de Leyer notice Snowman. He bought the grey ex-plow horse for $80 and trained him to be a jumper. Snowman became one of the best and most beloved show jumpers of all time.

Show Jumping Riders

Horses could not succeed in show-jumping events without the training, guidance, and skill of their riders. These pages show some of the legendary men and women of the show-jumping world.

Michael Matz is a show-jumping superstar. He rode a number of horses such as Jet Run, Chef, and The General. Matz won countless championships, including five gold medals at the Pan American Games. He competed for the United States at the 1976, 1992, and 1996 Olympic Games. He won a silver medal in the team event in 1996. In 2005, Matz was inducted into the Show Jumping Hall of Fame.

Michael Matz was the first equestrian ever chosen to carry the American flag at the opening and closing ceremonies of the Olympic Games.

In 1981, award-winning American rider Lisa Jacquin decided to train For the Moment. The Thoroughbred was going to be a short project until something better came along. For the Moment was a difficult horse to train. Jacquin continued to work with him.

In 1983, Jacquin entered For the Moment in his first big show-jumping competition. They won the event. Jacquin and For the Moment went on to compete together for several years. They became one of the most successful pairs in show-jumping history.

FACT BOX

The Show Jumping Hall of Fame is an organization that honors great moments and competitors in the sport of show jumping. So far, 45 people and 16 horses have been inducted into the Hall of Fame.

Horses and riders must work together to succeed in show jumping. Here Hall-of-Famer Abdullah carries his rider over a difficult jump.

Facts and Figures

Show-jumping competitions test riders and their horses. They must race harder, run faster, and jump higher. Some of the feats, facts, and figures of show jumping are shown on these pages.

The highest obstacle ever jumped in competition was over eight feet (2.47 m). It was completed in 1949 by a rider from Chile. His name was Captain Alberto Larraguibel Morales and his horse was called Huaso. The longest jump ever made was over 27.5 feet (8.40 m). It was completed by Andre Ferreira from South Africa and the horse

Something in 1975. Obstacles in standard show-jumping events must be no higher than 5.6 feet (1.7 m). Triple spreads can be no wider than 7.2 feet (2.2 m). All other spreads can be no wider than 6.6 feet (2 m). Water jumps must be no longer than 14.8 feet (4.5 m).

Hans Günter Winkler and his horse Halla have received the most medals in Olympic show-jumping history.

Germany has won more Olympic show-jumping events than any other country. It has won a whopping 81 medals! The United States has 49 Olympic medals, and Sweden has 41 medals. Hans Günter Winkler has won more Olympic medals in show jumping than any other rider. He competed in six Olympic Games from 1956 to 1976. He won five gold medals, one silver medal, and one bronze medal for Germany. Halla won more gold medals in Olympic show jumping than any other horse. The bay mare was ridden by Winkler. She won a total of three gold medals in individual and team events.

At the 2008 Olympics, the equestrian events were held in Hong Kong, China. All other events took place in Beijing.

Glossary

bay Describing a horse that is reddish-brown in color

equestrian Related to horses

FEI Fédération Equestre Internationale, the governing body of show jumping

pony A large hoofed animal that measures 14.2 hands or less

purse The amount of money the winner of a horse race receives

quarantine To keep people or animals separate from others for health reasons

seat The position a rider takes in the saddle

stamina The strength and energy to do something for long periods of time

stride The distance a horse covers in one step

warmbloods A group of horses that are bred to compete in sporting events

Index

breeds 18

care 19

clothing 24, 25

courses 4, 5, 6, 7, 8–9, 11, 12, 13, 20, 21, 22

cross-country 15

dressage 5, 15, 17, 19

eventing 15, 17

faults 13

Federico Caprilli 21

forward seat 21

Grand Prix 16, 19, 24, 25

grooming 19

ground poles 11, 18

Hall of Fame 27, 28, 29

jump-offs 13

jumps 4, 5, 6, 8, 9, 10–11, 12, 20, 21, 22

Olympic Games 9, 16, 17, 19, 26, 28, 30, 31

Puissance 15

scoring 5, 12–13

tack 22, 23

training 15, 18, 19, 21, 27, 28, 29

World Equestrian Games 16

Printed in the U.S.A.—CG